GOD'S SERVANT
JOB

A POEM WITH A PROMISE

DOUGLAS BOND
ILLUSTRATED BY TODD SHAFFER

PUBLISHING
P.O. BOX 817 • PHILLIPSBURG • NEW JERSEY 08865-0817

GOD LOVES JOB

In ancient times there was
   A blameless man from Uz—
An upright, wealthy man named Job,
   Who wore a turban and a robe.

Of all the men of the east
   This Job was far from the least;
With camels, donkeys, sheep, and herds,
   This man was rich in deeds and words.

Job daily for his children prayed,
   Lest one of them in sin had strayed,
And humbly had them purified,
   Lest one of them had cursed or lied.

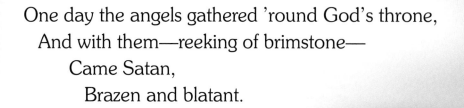

One day the angels gathered 'round God's throne,
  And with them—reeking of brimstone—
    Came Satan,
      Brazen and blatant.

Then God asked Satan,
  "From where have you arrived?"
The fallen fiend replied
  (While God's high throne he eyed),

"I come from roaming to and fro;
  With trouble, grief, and hate I sow
Decay, deceit, and dust, and woe;
  With pain and thirst and lust I go."

"Have you considered blameless Job?
Have you considered upright Job?
My evil-shunning servant Job?"

What man loves God for who God is?
Humph!
Job fears God for all God gives.

"Yes, but for nothing does Job fear?
    He's in it for the wealth, that's clear.
  Give Job this many sheep and herds?
    Of course he'll bow and keep Your words.
  Extend his wealth throughout the land?
    What man would turn and bite Your hand?
  But throw this favored Job down on the rack—
    He'll curse and swear and turn his back!"

"Then go," said God, "and take Job's wealth away,
    But on the man himself not a finger lay."

  Slavering with pleasure,
    Satan shrieked with delight.
  He tore from God's presence,
    On Job's wealth to alight.

Poor Job knew nothing of this trial
  (One that would last for quite a while).

Then suddenly a messenger appeared
  From where the oxen plowed.
"The Sabeans attacked!" he cried.
  "And all is lost!" he shrieked aloud.

Job sat stunned—then feared
  As another slave appeared:
"A blazing fire consumed your sheep,
  And I alone am left to weep!"

Another messenger appeared
  —Gasping for air,
    —Tearing his hair.

Another woe to hear?
  Poor Job recoiled with fear.

"Your house was struck by a whirling wind,
And, Job, your children were within,
  Entombed beneath the rubble.
    Oh, what woe, what trouble!"

Job tore his robe and shaved his head,
   Then fell upon his knees and said,

"Naked I came from my mother's womb—
   And naked will I lie down in my tomb.
O Lord, who gives and takes away—
   I'll bless You, Lord, though come what may."

In all he prayed Job did not sin
   (So Satan did not win),
      Nor charge the Lord with wrong for all of it,
         Nor stomp and rage or throw a fit.

Again around God's throne the angels bowed,
   And with them Satan lurked, so vile and proud.

"Observe," said God to the fiend.
   "My servant Job, as you can see,
     Still holds to his integrity."

"Skin for skin and bone for bone!
   Make Job sick and make Job moan.
Strike the man and do your worst,
   Then he'll squirm and writhe and curse."

"Take Job's health away—but beware:
   Don't take his life—oh, don't you dare!"

Slavering with pleasure,
   Satan shrieked with delight.
He tore from God's presence,
   On Job's health to alight.

Soon Job had boils and oozing pores—
    The neighbors' dogs licked his sores.

Poor Job collapsed amidst the trash;
    In pain, he sat on piles of ash;
With pieces from a broken pot,
    He scraped away at all the rot.

"My husband, why hold fast to God,
    Since He has struck you with His rod?
Since hope of all relief is gone,
    Oh, why—oh, goodness gracious—why
        Don't you curse your God and die?"

Job raised his head from the rubble:
    "Shall we accept good from our God—
        And not trouble?"

Job's Foolish Friends

Soon word got out, and from afar
Came Eliphaz the Temanite,
  With Bildad and his friend Zophar,
    All full of wise insight,
    All sure that they could put Job right.

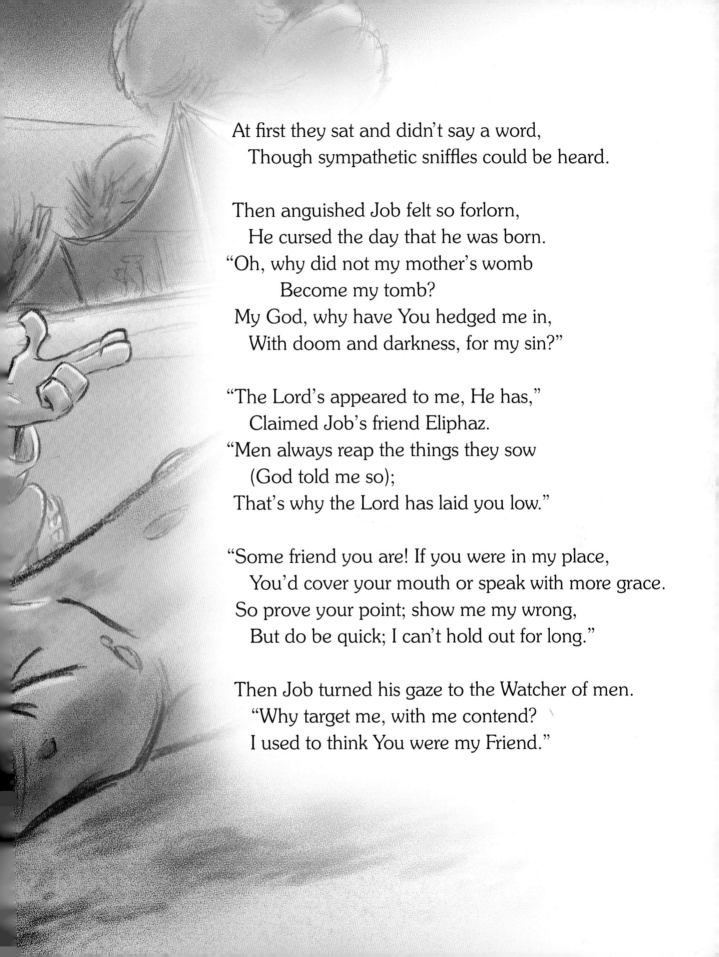

At first they sat and didn't say a word,
 Though sympathetic sniffles could be heard.

Then anguished Job felt so forlorn,
 He cursed the day that he was born.
"Oh, why did not my mother's womb
  Become my tomb?
My God, why have You hedged me in,
 With doom and darkness, for my sin?"

"The Lord's appeared to me, He has,"
 Claimed Job's friend Eliphaz.
"Men always reap the things they sow
 (God told me so);
That's why the Lord has laid you low."

"Some friend you are! If you were in my place,
 You'd cover your mouth or speak with more grace.
So prove your point; show me my wrong,
 But do be quick; I can't hold out for long."

Then Job turned his gaze to the Watcher of men.
 "Why target me, with me contend?
 I used to think You were my Friend."

Then Bildad interrupted poor Job's prayer:
    "Now hear me, Job; you'd best beware.
You pervert high justice; you are not fair!
    Are we like stupid cattle in your sight?
Your sniveling anger is not right.

"Why did the roof fall down on your kin?
    Because God caught you in your sin!
God likes the good but strikes the bad;
    That's why you're lying here so sad."

"All right, my friends, mock on, mock on.
 Since God my trial prolongs,
    I give up all restraint
        And issue my complaint.

"This bitterness of soul I hate—
    Would someone please come arbitrate?
I speak to God, but why won't He reply?
    O God, please turn Your face and
    let me die."

(I pause now in my verse
    To make this clear: Job did not curse;
        Though he did charge God with
        wrong for all of it,
            And stomp and rage a bit,
            And throw a fit.)

"Sit up, and I'll explain this mess you're in,"
   Said Zophar with a grin.
"Can Job, the witless one, deceive the wise?
   Wild donkeys, too, do right in their own eyes.
So why these troubles that won't end?
   Because of all the poor folks you offend,
Along with all that patience that you lack—
   Of course God's laid you on the rack!"

"Wait! Patience! Wait! Remember me:
　　I am righteous, can't you see?
I've made a covenant with my eyes—
　　I love the poor—and there's lots more.
In all this woe God is not wise.

"Yet though He slay me I'll still hope—
　　I'm sure it's all a big mistake.
I raise my voice, I call, I grope—
　　It's my poor life that's now at stake!
But God is silent while I ache.

"One day I'll breathe my final breath,
　　And my frail life will end in death;
Yet in my flesh, by sovereign grace,
　　I'll see my Savior face to face.

"Yet now I'm cursed—it's so unfair!
　　The Watcher high up there—
　　　　Does He still care?"

A Wise, Young Friend

Next came a friend named Elihu.
"Poor Job, I've got to speak to you,
   But since I am so young,
      I thought it best to hold my tongue.
Yet now a word I will attempt,
   Though what I say brings your contempt.
Job's friends, you've babbled on so long,
   But none of you has proved Job wrong.

"This Job complains that God ignores his words,
    That God denies the justice he deserves.
  Against the Lord you multiply your words,
    But, Job, it's not on your terms God rewards.
  This high Creator God who rules and guides,
    He roars and storms—and on the whirlwind rides.
  He does all this without consulting you;
    What more do you think God should do?

"His works, His plans, His power, His might
    Are always perfect, just, and right.
  Redeeming mercy gives us light,
    The light alone that gives us sight,
      And songs of joy within the night.

"He ransoms us and pays our debt;
    Our souls He rescues from the pit.
  His ways are wondrous, high above,
    Of mercy, kindness, and of love.
  This righteous God's so full of grace,
    My trembling heart leaps from its place!"

Before poor Job could make reply,
    The voice of God came from the sky.

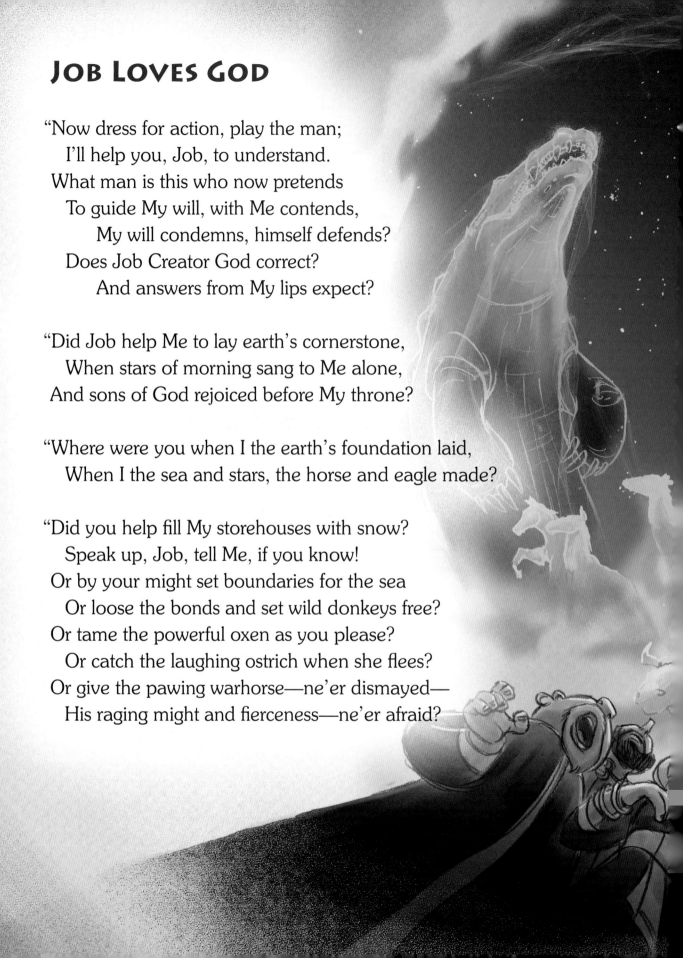

JOB LOVES GOD

"Now dress for action, play the man;
   I'll help you, Job, to understand.
What man is this who now pretends
   To guide My will, with Me contends,
     My will condemns, himself defends?
Does Job Creator God correct?
     And answers from My lips expect?

"Did Job help Me to lay earth's cornerstone,
   When stars of morning sang to Me alone,
And sons of God rejoiced before My throne?

"Where were you when I the earth's foundation laid,
   When I the sea and stars, the horse and eagle made?

"Did you help fill My storehouses with snow?
   Speak up, Job, tell Me, if you know!
Or by your might set boundaries for the sea
   Or loose the bonds and set wild donkeys free?
Or tame the powerful oxen as you please?
   Or catch the laughing ostrich when she flees?
Or give the pawing warhorse—ne'er dismayed—
   His raging might and fierceness—ne'er afraid?

"Now dress for action, play the man;
　I'll help you, Job, to understand.
　　Consider the Leviathan,
With fearsome teeth and scales like shields.
　Buy him? Spear him? To none he yields.
　Snorting, thrashing, breathing fire—
　　Touch him? Pet him? Raise his ire.

"Leviathans are Mine and so are you;
　To save yourself what can you do?
You, Job, demand to know the reasons why—
　Condemning God, yourself to justify.

"Devoid of knowledge and of skill,
　Job moans and fumes and doubts My will.
If I guide all without your aid,
　And by My power all things have made,
Why then My will do you degrade
　And whine that you are underpaid?
My high decree does Job invade?
　In things too deep you've tried to wade."

"My troubles made me feel so sore—
    Yes, twice I spoke but now no more.
Yes, answers once I did demand;
    Now on my mouth I place my hand.

"O God, I will be silent now
    And speak no more of how
Or why You rule the universe.
    I got things wrong—all in reverse.

"Before I'd only faintly heard,
    But now I see Your face
        And heed Your Holy Word
            And hope in Your sweet grace.
My Lord, in dust and ashes I repent
    For my despairing argument."

"My servant Job has seen the light,
But you, his friends, got nothing right.
Now go to Job and he will pray;
At his feet your offerings lay.
My patient son and friend I'll hear,
And for his sake your sins I'll clear."

With gifts Job's loved ones came to feast,
  His brothers, sisters, from the east;
And God His bounteous treasures poured,
  On Job His righteousness restored.
With seven sons, and daughters fair,
  He made each one of them his heir.

Then Job, through trouble, loss, and tears,
  Whom God in grace and mercy tried,
    Lived many full and happy years
      Before he died.

JOB'S GREAT REDEEMER!

I know that my Redeemer lives!
And with His life my sin forgives.
O Jesus, Lord, I'll hope and pray,
And patient be—though come what may.

When troubles come with grief and tears,
And hope is lost in all my fears,
On God who gives and takes away
My sins and doubts and sorrows lay.

His ways are wondrous, high above,
So full of righteousness and love.
So glorious is my God of grace,
My longing heart leaps from its place.

Redeeming mercy gives me light
And songs of joy within the night.
Since Jesus all my troubles bore,
I am God's friend forevermore!

O great Redeemer, glorious sight!
Your will and ways are always right.
My heart within me yearns to see
Your glory, light, and majesty!

BIG WORDS (LIKE "UZ")

Anguish: *noun*. What you feel when your body and mind are in real trouble.

Arbitrate: *verb*. When two people have not been getting along and you help them to become friends.

Bounteous: *adjective*. Extravagant, without limit.

Dismay: *noun*. What you feel when you have to face a big problem.

Fiend: *noun*. Another name for a demon or for the Devil himself.

Forlorn: *adjective*. Hopeless.

Integrity: *noun*. What you have when you do what is right even when it hurts you.

Lest: *adverb*. For fear that.

Leviathan: *noun*. A really big, scary sea monster.

Patience: *noun*. What Jesus had when He endured ultimate suffering on the cross without complaining.

Righteousness: *noun*. An attribute of God Himself, who alone is and does what is right and just. Jesus Christ is the righteousness of Job and all believers by the free grace of the gospel (Philippians 3:9).

Sabeans: *noun*. Ancient people from present-day Yemen.

Temanite: *noun*. Another name for an Edomite, a member of a Palestinian people descended from Esau.

Uz: *noun*. Ancient near-eastern region, today in western Jordan or southern Syria.

QUIZ

1. What did God say to Satan about Job (Job 1:8)?
2. At the beginning of the story, what were some of the bad things that happened to Job?
3. How did Job respond at first to the bad things that came into his life (1:20–22)?
4. How did Satan say Job would respond to bad things in his life (1:11; 2:4–5)?
5. According to Job's foolish friends, why did God bring bad things into Job's life (11:6b)? Compare that with what God said about Job (1:8).
6. What did Job learn about God and the bad things that had happened in his life?
7. What did God say to Job's foolish friends (42:7–8)?

LET'S THINK!

1. What are some bad things that have happened to you or your family members?
2. Have you ever been impatient and complained about bad things?
3. Romans 8:28 sounds almost like the book of Job in one verse. Read this verse and discuss it together.
4. When God came down and met with Job and spoke to him (42:1–6), what did Job do with his hand and his mouth?
5. In almost the exact middle of the book of Job (19:25–26), Job makes his confession of faith. Now read together Job 33:23–30 and compare Elihu's words with what Job confessed in the middle of the scroll.
6. What can we learn from the hymn "Job's Great Redeemer!"?

For Amelia, Gwenna, Giles, and Gillian;
Brittany and Jesse; Rhodric and Victoria;
Cedric and Ashley; Desmond and Shauna

In loving memory of my father, Douglas Elwood Bond (1933–2006),
who, while I wrote *God's Servant Job,* patiently suffered with the
cancer that would take his life.

ISBN: 978-1-59638-734-8 (pbk)
ISBN: 978-1-59638-735-5 (ePub)
ISBN: 978-1-59638-736-2 (Mobi)

Printed in the United States of America

Library of Congress Control Number: 2015944891

God asks Satan a question:
"Have you considered my servant Job?"

What happens next turns Job's world upside down. What will God's servant Job do when hardship strikes? Will Job keep loving God? Will God rescue Job?

Learn from the oldest book in the Bible as Job teaches us how to be faithful in the hard times that we face. Best of all, find out how God's story reveals our Redeemer, Jesus.

INCLUDES DISCUSSION QUESTIONS

DOUGLAS BOND is the author of a number of books of historical fiction and biography. He and his wife have two daughters and four sons. Bond is an elder in the Presbyterian Church of America, a teacher, a conference speaker, and a leader of church history tours. Visit his website at www.bondbooks.net.

TODD SHAFFER is an animation director and character animator who has worked on almost one hundred projects, from commercials to feature films. Cofounder of Glorious Films, he wrote and directed *The Promise: Birth of the Messiah*.

P&R
PUBLISHING
www.prpbooks.com

CHILDREN / NON-FICTION
ISBN: 978-1-59638-734-8

EAN

9 781596 387348

50999